Little Bo Illustrates

The Art of WAR

By Sun Tzu

L. H. Draken
Anastasiia Kuusk

This book is not a historical text or intended as a direct
translation of the original Sun Tzu work. The translations are
based on the works of Lionel Giles (1875), now available in
the public domain.

To my sons —
May you learn to win your battles before they are fought.

- LHD

是故勝兵先勝而後求戰，

敗兵先戰而後求勝。

You are slated for defeat if you fight
first and afterward look for victory.

孫子曰：

兵者，國之大事。

死生之地，存亡之道，不可不察也。

故經之以五，校之以計，而索其情。

Therefore,
the art of war is of vital importance
to the State.

It is a matter of life and death,
a road either to safety or to ruin.

Thus it is a subject of study
that can, under no circumstances, be neglected.

Sun Tzu says:
If you know the enemy and know
yourself, you need not fear the result of a
hundred battles.

If you know yourself but not the enemy,
for every victory gained you will also
suffer a defeat.

If you know neither the enemy nor
yourself, you will succumb in every battle.

故曰：

知己知彼，百戰不殆；

不知彼而知己，一勝一負；

不知彼不知己，戰必殆。

善用兵者，

修道而保法，

故能為勝敗之政。

12

The consummate leader cultivates the moral law,
and strictly adheres to method and discipline.
Thus it is in his power to control success.

Only the person who completely
understands the evils of war
can thoroughly understand the best way
of carrying it out.

•

In war, the way is to avoid what is strong
and to strike at what is weak

兵之形，避實而擊虛。

故不盡知用兵之害者，

則不能盡知用兵之利也。

15

The use of chaos to confuse the enemy
requires perfect discipline;

The use of fear to trap the enemy
requires extreme courage;

The use of weakness to make your
enemy over confident requires extreme
strength.

亂生于治,
怯生于勇,
弱生于強。

掠郷分眾，廊地分利。

When you plunder a countryside,
let the spoil be divided amongst your men;
when you capture new territory, cut it up
into allotments for the benefit of the
soldiery.

Think of your soldiers as your own flesh and blood,
and they will follow you to the deepest valley;
regard them as your own sons, and they will stand by
you till death.

視卒如嬰兒，故可與之赴深谿；
視卒如愛子，故可與之死。

故令之以文，齊之以武，是謂必取。

Soldiers must be treated in the first
instance with humanity,
but kept under control by means of
iron discipline.

This is a certain road to victory.

以虞待不虞者勝。

If a general shows confidence in his men but
always insists on his orders being obeyed,
the gain will be mutual.

知可以戰與不可以戰者勝。

He will win who knows when to fight and
when not to fight.

懸權而動。

勝可知，而不可為。

One may know how to conquer
without being able to do it.

•

Ponder and deliberate before you
make a move.

難知如陰,動如雷震。

Attack him where he is unprepared,
appear where you are not expected.

是故屈諸侯者以害,役諸侯者以業,趨諸
侯者以利。

Cut down hostile chiefs by inflicting
damage on them;
make trouble for them, and keep them
constantly engaged;
hold out deceptive temptations
and make them rush to do your bidding.

善守者，藏于九地之下；

善攻者，動于九天之上。

故能自保而全勝也。

The general who is skilled in defense hides
in the most secret recesses of the earth;
he who is skilled in attack flashes forth
from the topmost heights of heaven.

Let your plans be dark and impenetrable as night,
and when you move, fall like a thunderbolt.

難知如陰，動如雷震。

無約而請和者，謀也。

Peace proposals unaccompanied by a
sworn covenant indicate a plot.

利而誘之，亂而取之。

勝者之戰民也，若決積水於千例之谿者，形也。

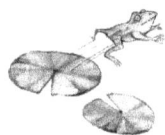

Hold out baits to entice the enemy.
Feign disorder and crush him.

•

The onrush of a conquering force is
like the bursting of dammed waters into
a chasm a thousand miles deep.
Tactical positions go by the wayside.

敵則能戰之，
少則能逃之，
不若則能避之。

If equally matched, we can offer battle;
If slightly inferior in numbers,
we can avoid the enemy;
If quite unequal in every way,
we can flee from him.

孫子曰：

昔之善戰者，

先為不可勝，以待敵之可勝。

Sun Tzŭ said:
The good fighters of old first put
themselves beyond the possibility of
defeat, and then waited for an
opportunity of defeating the enemy.

不可勝在己，可勝在敵。

To secure ourselves against defeat lies in our own hands, but the opportunity of defeating the enemy is provided by the enemy himself.

歸師勿遏。

Do not interfere with an army that is
returning home.

•

不可勝在己,可勝在敵。

In war, then, let your great object be victory,
not lengthy campaigns.

敵近而靜者,恃其險也。

When the enemy is close at hand
and remains quiet,
he is relying on the natural strength
of his position.

•

以虞待不虞者勝

He will win who, prepared himself,
waits to take the enemy unprepared.

故舉秋毫不為多力，
見日月不為明目，
聞雷鍾不為聰耳。
古之所謂善戰者，
勝勝易勝者也。

To see sun and moon
is no sign of sharp sight;
to hear the noise of thunder
is no sign of quick ear.
What the ancients called a clever fighter
is one who not only wins,
but excels in winning with ease.

圍師遺闕,窮寇勿迫。

When you surround an army, leave an outlet free.
Do not press a desperate foe too hard.

•

能因敵變化而取勝者,謂之神。

He who can modify his tactics in relation to his
opponent and thereby succeed in winning,
may be called a heaven-born captain.

•

夫惟無慮而易敵者,必擒於人。

He who exercises no forethought but makes light
of his opponents is sure to be captured by them.

故戰道必勝,主曰無戰,必戰可也;
戰道不勝,主曰必戰,無戰可也。

If fighting is sure to result in victory, then
you must fight, even though the ruler
forbid it;
if fighting will not result in victory, then
you must not fight even at the ruler's
bidding.

●

將能而君不御者勝。

He will win who has military capacity and
is not interfered with by the sovereign.

塗有所不由，

軍有所不擊，

城有所不攻，

地有所不爭，

君命有所不受。

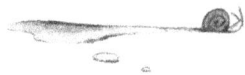

56

There are roads that must not be followed,
armies that must not be attacked,
towns that must not be besieged,
positions that must not be contested,
commands of the sovereign that must not be
obeyed.

齊勇若一，政之道也。

我不欲戰，畫地而守之。敵不得與我戰者，乖其所之也。

If we do not wish to fight, we can
prevent the enemy from engaging us
even though the lines of our
encampment be merely traced out on
the ground.
All we need to do is to throw
something unexpected in his way.

•

The principle on which to manage an
army is to set up one standard of
courage which all must reach.

If he is secure at all points,
be prepared for him.
If he is in superior strength, evade him.

實而備之，強而避之。

Hence, though an obstinate fight may
be made by a small force,
in the end it must be captured by the
larger force.

故小敵之堅,大敵之擒也。

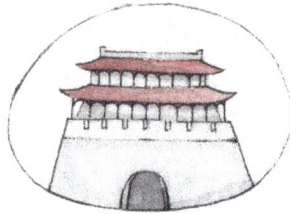

Thus the highest form of generalship is
to baulk the enemy's plans;
the next best is to prevent the junction
of the enemy's forces;
and the worst policy of all
is to besiege walled cities.

故上兵伐謀，

其次伐交，

其次伐兵，

下政攻城。

角之而知有餘不足之處。

Carefully compare the opposing army with your own, so that you may know where strength is superabundant and where it is deficient.

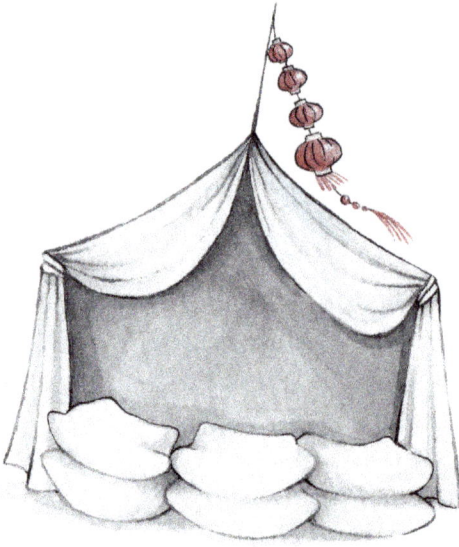

故善用兵者, 屈人之兵而非戰也。
拔人之城而非攻也, 人之國而非久也。

The skillful leader subdues the enemy's
troops
without any fighting;

he captures their cities
without laying siege to them;

he overthrows their kingdom
without lengthy operations in the field.

Hence to fight and conquer in all your
battles is not supreme excellence;
supreme excellence consists in breaking
the enemy's resistance without fighting.

是故百戰百勝，非善之善者也；不戰而屈人之兵，善之善者也。

Sun Tzŭ said:
In the practical art of war, the best thing of all
is to take the enemy's country whole and intact;
to shatter and destroy it is not helpful.

孫子曰:凡用兵之法,
全國為上,破國次之;
全軍為上,破軍次之。

If, in the midst of difficulties, we are always
ready to seize an advantage,
we may extricate ourselves from misfortune.

雜于害，而患可解也。

The art of war teaches us to rely not on the
likelihood of the enemy's not coming,
but on our own readiness to receive him;
not on the chance of his not attacking, but
rather on the facts that have made our
position unassailable.

故用兵之法，無恃其不來，恃吾有以待也；無恃其不攻，恃吾有所不可攻也。

To my sons,

It is the natural instinct of every good parent, as soon as their infant child enters the world, to protect their child from the dangers of the universe.

There is no moment in a persons life when they are more vulnerable to the mere fact of existence than the first weeks of life, thus this instinct to protect has probably been paramount in the furthering of the species.

But as natural and important as this role as guardian is, it is not the *fundamental* role of a parent.

I wish my only role was to protect you, my children; I would build a concrete bunker under which to hide you away. There would be an airlock system for food delivery and fresh water would be pumped through a reverse osmosis double filtration system, spiked with Vitamin D supplements and necessary vitamins. You would be safe from the dangers of the world and the universe and I would have you forever near.

Perhaps I would succeed in protecting you, in some sick way, but I would have failed at my job as your parent. (And probably be committed to an insane asylum or life in prison; for good reason.)

The psychologist Dr. D. W. Winnicot said that the good mother necessarily fails. I think this is true. As your parent, I must only protect you from what you cannot protect yourself. I must not only protect you but also gradually remove my protection and expose you to greater and greater danger, until you are strong enough to face existence on your own. My job is not to sequester you from the world, but to strengthen you to one day be the noble knight, who stands upright with his shoulders back and head held high in the face of danger, not because he doesn't know the risks of engagement, but because he knows the risks and has chosen to voluntarily face them anyway.

I cannot do that by keeping you from the danger. What I can do is make you strong, so you are a match to the worlds dragons.

I want you to conquer the god of temptation and not eat gummy bears for dinner *so that you* will live a healthy life and not suffer in hospital more than necessary.

I want you to fight the dragon of chaos and make your bed and keep your room tidy, *so that* the routine of your life will be characterized by order and you will be able to do important work.

I want you to get your homework done on time and to learn to relish acquiring knowledge, so that you will be able to cultivate whatever new skills you will need for each stage of life.

I want to show you how to live in the mystical land of a good book, so that you will be steeped in the mythology and wisdom of the wise men who already conquered the leviathans of old.

And I want you to say please and thank you, so that you will learn to treat others with the God-given respect they deserve as beings harboring their own spark of divinity.

I must prepare you to act independently and with nobility in the world. To one day leave the home that we as your parents made for you, and to go to out into the unknown. To conquer your dragons, to rescue those who cannot rescue themselves, and perhaps if you're so lucky, to one day have your own family.

I hope your childhood is characterized by action—by practicing to act in the world when the consequences of a wrong decision are a time out or a forfeited dessert, so that when the stakes are high, you will be strong enough to do what is noble, even if that is also what is most dangerous.

Half of **Anastasiia Kuusk's** blood consists of watercolor, which might explain her dedication to the art. She reads, runs and watches her favorite series, but most of all she paints. When immersed in a project, she will often live the life of a hermit, sometimes not leaving the house for weeks at a time. Anastasiia is in love with Asia and enjoys traveling through lands with incomprehensible languages.

If you loved the paintings in this book, follow her on Instagram, @Anastasiia_kuusk_art, where her husband does his best to censor her natural transparency. Despite his best efforts, some of the family secrets still make it to the social-media public.

. . .

L. H. Draken spends much of her time killing characters in her mysteries and trying to get away with it. Her last book, *The Year of the Rabid Dragon*, was set in Beijing, China. Sometimes she gets herself into other projects, like this —finding new ways to inspire her children.

Lawrence lives in Munich with her husband, two sons and their teddy bears. Find her on Instagram, @lhdraken, and online at www.lhdraken.com.

www.ingramcontent.com/pod-product-compliance
Lightning Source LLC
Chambersburg PA
CBHW041826090426
42811CB00010B/1119